THRILLING THEME PARKS

HERSHEYPARK

BY MONIKA DAVIES

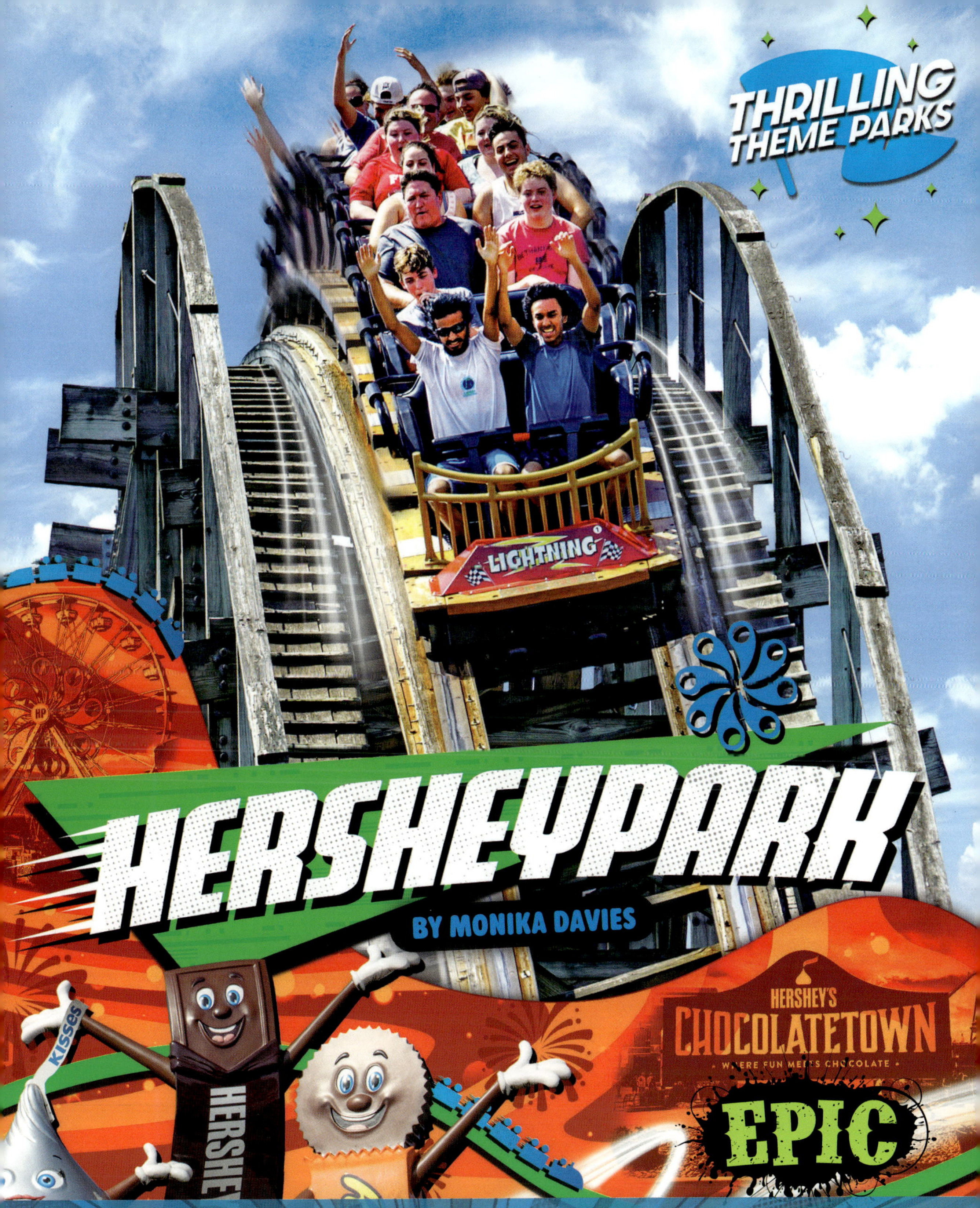

EPIC

EPIC, AN IMPRINT OF BELLWETHER MEDIA BY FLUTTERBEE

EPIC

EPIC BOOKS are no ordinary books. They burst with intense action, high-speed heroics, and shadows of the unknown. Are you ready for an Epic adventure?

This edition first published in 2027 by Bellwether Media, Inc.

For information regarding permission, write to Bellwether Media, Inc., Attention: Permissions Department, 3500 American Blvd W, Suite 150, Bloomington, MN 55431.

Library of Congress Cataloging-in-Publication Data

Names: Davies, Monika author
Title: Hersheypark / Monika Davies.
Description: Minneapolis, Minnesota : Bellwether Media, Inc, 2027. | Series: Thrilling theme parks | Includes bibliographical references and index. | Audience: Ages 8-12 | Audience: Grades 4-6 | Summary: "Engaging images accompany information about Hersheypark. The combination of high-interest subject matter and light text is intended for students in grades 2 through 7"--Provided by publisher Provided by publisher.
Identifiers: LCCN 2026011445 (print) | LCCN 2026011446 (ebook) | ISBN 9798898801038 library binding | ISBN 9798898802271 ebook
Subjects: LCSH: Hersheypark (Hershey, Pa.)--History | Amusement parks--Pennsylvania--Hershey--History | Hershey, Milton Snavely, 1857-1945
Classification: LCC GV1853.3.P42 D38 2027 (print) | LCC GV1853.3.P42 (ebook) | DDC 791.06/874818--dc23/eng/20260313
LC record available at https://lccn.loc.gov/2026011445
LC ebook record available at https://lccn.loc.gov/2026011446

Editor: Elizabeth Neuenfeldt Designer: Gabriel Hilger

Printed in the United States of America, North Mankato, MN.

TABLE OF CONTENTS

THE SWEETEST PLACE ON EARTH

A parent and child sit next to each other. Their cart slowly climbs the track. They **squeeze** each other's hands.

Whoosh! They are speeding down the Lightning Racer. They scream with delight! It is a exciting day at Hersheypark.

LIGHTNING RACER
LIGHTNING

Hersheypark opened in 1906. It is in Hershey, Pennsylvania.

HERSHEYPARK MAP

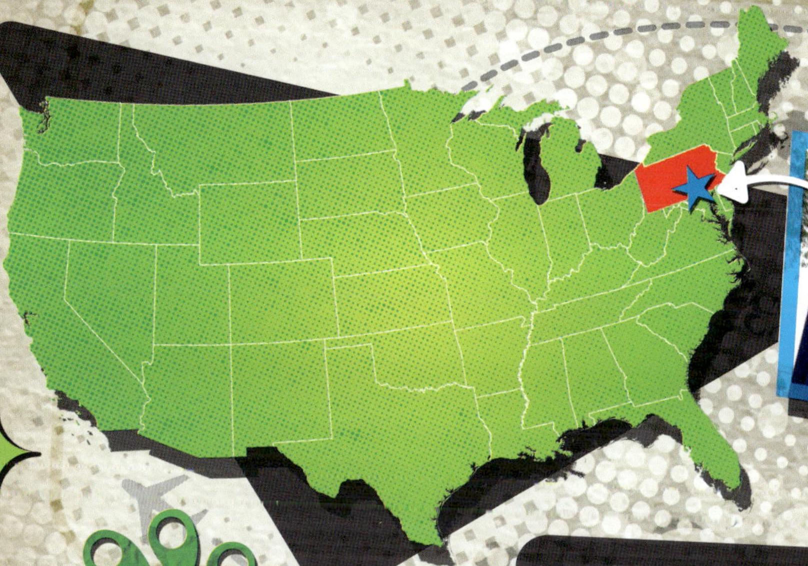

The park was first built for workers at the Hershey chocolate factory. They had picnics and went boating. Now, the park is full of exciting rides.

THE MAKING OF HERSHEYPARK

BORN 1857

ROLE

Founder of Hershey Company and Hersheypark

ACCOMPLISHMENTS

Helped create the Hershey bar and build a school for young boys without parents

MILTON S. HERSHEY

Milton S. Hershey started the Hershey Chocolate Company in 1894. He sold his first chocolate bars in 1900. They were popular!

The company needed to **expand**. Milton decided to build a new factory. He picked a spot in Pennsylvania.

Milton built a town around the factory. He wanted workers to enjoy their lives outside of work.

He added a local park called Hershey Park. At first, the park hosted picnics and baseball games.

Soon, the park began to grow. Milton added a merry-go-round and a pool to its **attractions**.

A GREEN COMET

The Comet opened in 1946. The wooden roller coaster was first painted green. Milton wanted it to match the park's green space.

Over the years, more rides were added. Fast roller coasters shot people around a track. Ferris wheels spun in circles.

In the 1970s, Hershey Park became Hersheypark. New areas were added. Pioneer Frontier opened in 1984.

Midway America opened in 1996. It featured a new wooden roller coaster called the Wildcat!

WILDCAT'S REVENGE

In 2022, the Wildcat coaster closed. Wildcat's Revenge opened the next year! The new ride is made of wood and steel.

THE WILDCAT

Hersheypark Attendance Records

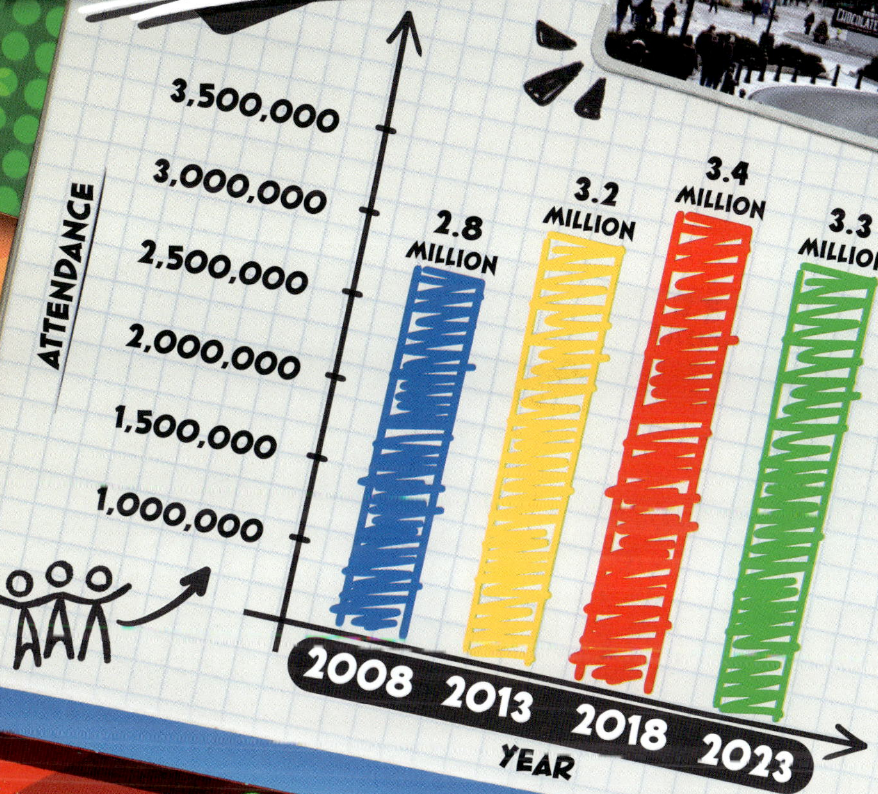

HERSHEY PARK IN THE 1950S

HERSHEYPARK TODAY

There are seven **themed** areas at Hersheypark. Visitors first enter Hershey's Chocolatetown. It is the newest area of the park. It opened in 2020.

Chocolatetown honors Milton's story. Everything is chocolate themed!

CANDYMONIUM

WHAT IS IT?

Hersheypark's tallest, fastest, and longest roller coaster

STAT

It is almost **2.5** minutes long.

FUN FACT

It is called "The World's Sweetest Coaster."

People can eat funnel cakes in Founder's Way. Crowds line up for roller coasters in the Hollow.

TWIZZLERS TWISTED GRAVITY

Twizzlers Twisted Gravity is a giant swing. It swings riders at fast speeds. It opened in 2025!

Kissing Tower offers a bird's-eye view of the park. Visitors race down waterslides at the Boardwalk.

HERSHEYPARK EVENTS

Hersheypark Halloween is in the fall. People enter haunted houses. Kids can follow the park's trick-or-treat trail.

Christmas Candylane

DATE

November to early January

EVENT

Visitors see reindeer and holiday lights.

Favorite park **souvenirs** include chocolate-themed plush characters. Everyone has a sweet time at Hersheypark!

Glossary

attractions—interesting things that people want to see or visit

expand—to become bigger

souvenirs—things people keep as reminders of places they visited

squeeze—to hold tightly

themed—related to the subject or idea on which the style of something is based

To Learn More

AT THE LIBRARY

Davies, Monika. *Knott's Berry Farm.* Minneapolis, Minn.: Bellwether Media, 2027.

Romero, Libby. *Amusement Park.* New York, N.Y.: DK Publishing, 2023.

Rusick, Jessica. *Amusement Parks: Then and Now.* Minneapolis, Minn.: Abdo Publishing, 2024.

ON THE WEB

FACTSURFER

Factsurfer.com gives you a safe, fun way to find more information.

1. Go to www.factsurfer.com.

2. Enter "Hersheypark" into the search box and click .

3. Select your book cover to see a list of related content.

Index

The images in this book are reproduced through the courtesy of: George Sheldon/ Alamy Stock Photo, front cover, p. 1; Jaclyn Vernace, front cover, pp. 1, 4; Lee, front cover, p. 1; Ritu Manoj Jethani, front cover, pp. 1, 12; Wirestock Creators, pp. 2-3; George Sheldon, pp. 3, 5, 16; Roy Johnson/ Alamy Stock Photo, p. 6; CNMages/ Alamy Stock Photo, p. 7; Everett Collection Inc/ Alamy Stock Photo, p. 8; PJ McDonnell, p. 8 (inset); Niday Picture Library/ Alamy Stock Photo, p. 9; Historic Collection/ Alamy Stock Photo, p. 10; 995577823Xyn/ Wikimedia Commons, p. 11; Joe Shlabotnik/ Flickr, pp. 13, 14, 18-19; Nathan Yeagle, pp. 15 (attendance), 21; Brian Retroland U.S.A./ Flickr, p. 15 (Hershey Park in the 1950s); Scott Smith/ Flickr, p. 17 (Candymonium); Anthony G. Reyes/ Flickr, p. 17 (sign); ConnellyCreative, p. 20; Viktorua, p. 20 (candy canes).